Who were the Celts?

The Celts were people who lived in western Europe. We think they were living there from about 700 BC.

Greeks and Romans knew the Celts as excitable people. The warriors in their tribes were tall, fair-haired and fierce.

They invaded Italy in the 5th century BC and even destroyed the capital city of Rome. The Celts also invaded other parts of Europe, as the arrows on the map show.

The Celts were famous for their beautiful metalwork and colourful clothes. There are lots of examples in this book.

MW00983672

Find
unsc
moc
on t

ANDIREL
NAITBRI
TUROPLAG
PAINS
CANREF
DSNWAILTREZ
TALIY
MANYREG
MEGLIUB
LOOSEZAKVIACCH
GHUNRAY

DANLOP
IANMARO
RIAGULAB
SAUTAIR
VIAGUASLOY
CREGEE
S.U.R.S.
KUTREY
NANDERTHELS
KENMARD
ABALANI

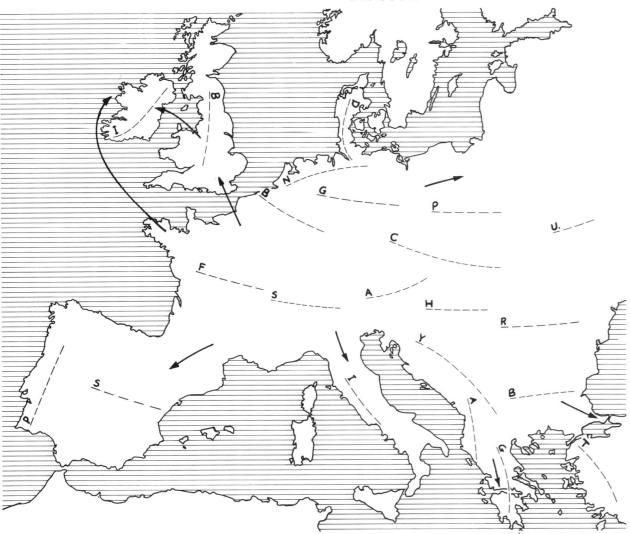

This is how the Celts pictured themselves: a carved head found in Czechoslovakia.

1

Celtic warriors

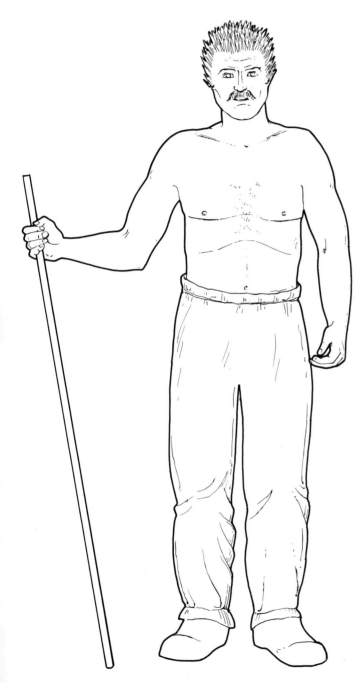

One ancient writer said that the Celtic people were 'mad keen on war, full of spirit and quick to begin a fight'. They tried to make themselves look frightening by combing their hair with lime to make it stand up on end like a porcupine's quills.

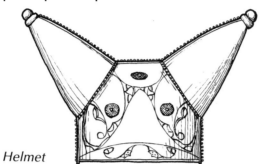

Helmet

Look at the front cover of this book. A battle is taking place outside a Celtic hill-top town. The Celtic warriors, often stripped to the waist or sometimes completely naked, rushed shouting into battle. The noise was increased by the tall animal-headed trumpet called a *carnyx*.

Women could be warriors too. The most famous is Queen Boudica (see page 15). One Roman writer described her as 'a very big woman, terrifying to look at. She had a harsh voice and wore her great mass of hair the colour of a lion's mane right down to her hips. She always wore a richly coloured tunic, a thick cloak fastened with a brooch and a large necklace of twisted gold around her neck.' You can see clothes and jewellery like the ones Boudica wore on pages 8 and 9.

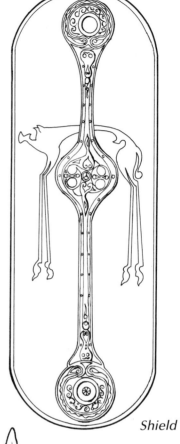

Shield

Spear-head

BATTLE WEAPONS
On this page you can see the weapons that warriors would carry in battle. Sometimes they wore helmets.

Sword

WARPAINT
Celtic men liked to decorate their bodies. Sometimes they were tattooed, and sometimes they painted patterns on their skins with a blue dye made from a plant called *woad*.

Draw these weapons in the right places on the warrior. Add some warpaint on his body. Colour him in.

Make your own helmet

The Celtic helmet on the opposite page was found over 100 years ago, in the River Thames near Waterloo Bridge in London. It is made of bronze and is the only horned helmet that survives from the Celtic world. Perhaps it was lost in a battle, or by a warrior crossing the river. Or was it an offering to the gods? (See page 12.)

To make a full-size helmet you will need a piece of paper or thin cardboard twice the size of this page. Each square on this page measures 1 centimetre across. Rule out the squares with a pencil, making each one 2 centimetres across.

Copy the helmet pieces carefully, and then rub out the squares. Colour the pieces to look like bronze.

Cut out the pieces very carefully. First fold flap A along the dotted line and stick it with glue or sticky tape to the other edge marked A. Now do the same with flap B. Make this part of the helmet like a hat, and then try it on.

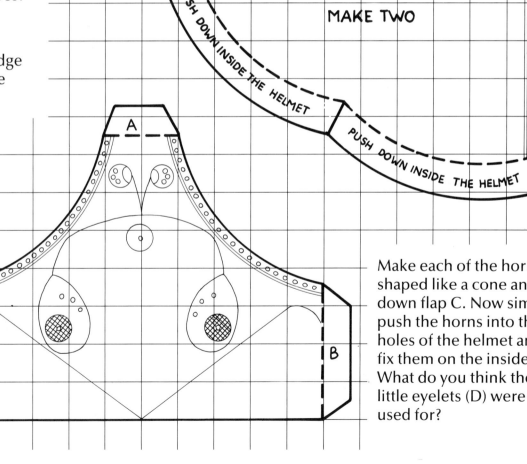

C

PUSH DOWN INSIDE THE HELMET

PUSH DOWN INSIDE THE HELMET

MAKE TWO

C

Make each of the horns shaped like a cone and fix down flap C. Now simply push the horns into the holes of the helmet and fix them on the inside. What do you think the little eyelets (D) were used for?

A

A

B

B

D

D

Celtic life

We know quite a lot about the Celtic peoples in Britain from archaeological excavations. The Celts were farmers. They lived on small farms, or in farming settlements of just a few houses, or in hill-top towns. We call these towns *hill-forts* because they were fortified (defended) with deep ditches, great banks of earth and walls of wood. You can see one on the front cover of this book.

Celtic houses were usually made of wood, with thatch or reeds on the roof. The wooden walls were covered with *daub* (a mixture of clay, straw, animal hair and dung) to keep out the weather.

In some parts of Britain the houses had stone walls. In the north and west of Scotland some people lived in *brochs*. These were very tall circular houses which protected them against being attacked.

Broch

Spot the deliberate mistakes! There are two things in this picture which should not be there. *Clue*: one is an animal which was not brought to Britain until much later. (Answer on page 16.)

Opposite is a picture of the inside of a Celtic house for you to colour.

There were always lots of things going on inside a Celtic house. The family lived here, cooked and stored food and other possessions here. On the right there is a *loom* for weaving the colourful Celtic woollen cloth. The little girl is spinning *yarn* ready for the loom.

Cooking and eating

Celtic farmers used oxen to plough their fields. The Celtic plough, which was really just a sharp piece of wood pulled through the soil, is called an *ard*.

The Celts grew a great variety of different crops in their fields. Here are some of them.

Emmer Wheat
(on a Celtic coin)

Cereals used for bread, porridge, or in stews

Spelt Wheat

Flax. Linen cloth was made from the stalks; animals ate the leaves; and oil was made from the seeds.

ANIMALS

Celtic peoples also kept a variety of animals. They ate meat from cows, goats, pigs and perhaps chickens. We know they kept sheep too, but probably for their wool and their milk rather than for meat. There were dogs around the villages. They must have helped to hunt animals like wild boar, which Celts were very fond of. The Celts also hunted and trapped wild birds, and probably kept bees. They also bred horses for riding.

Celtic Bean, used as a vegetable

The Celts also ate a number of plants (such as one called Fat Hen) which some people call weeds today. The stomach of an actual Celtic man who was discovered in a peat bog in Cheshire was so well preserved that archaeologists were able to work out what he had for his last meal. They found Emmer and Spelt Wheat, Barley, Fat Hen, Dock and Cow Parsley.

IN CELTIC TIMES

CELTIC COOKING

To make simple Celtic bread take some stone-ground or wholemeal wheat flour and mix it with barley flour (called *bere flour*) if you can get it from a wholefood shop. If you can't get bere flour, use just wholemeal flour.

Make sure a grown-up is there when you use the kitchen.
Mix 100 grams of flour with 5 tablespoons of water, until it makes a stiff paste. Shape this dough into small flat rounds.

Under a very hot grill, cook them for 2-3 minutes on each side. If you have a griddle or a heavy frying-pan, try cooking the bread that way, in just a little fat.

TODAY

Celtic clothes and jewellery

Look at the colourful clothes the Celtic warriors are wearing on the front cover of this book. They dyed the yarn in bright colours before weaving their patterned cloth.

They used natural ingredients to make the colours. For example, if they wanted brown, they used bark from a birch tree. The bark of the elder tree made black. Red and orange came from the root of goose-grass, and wild berries (such as elderberries) made blue.

Can you remember the name of another dye which the Celts used?

The decorated back of a mirror. The side you saw your reflection in was made of polished bronze.

Necklace made from coloured beads

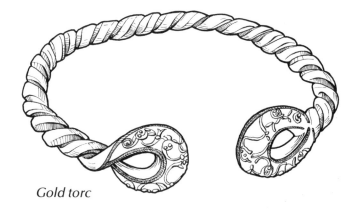

Gold torc

Celtic women, and men too, liked to wear jewellery. They wore rings on their toes as well as on their fingers, bracelets and armbands, neckbands called *torcs*, and necklaces.

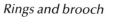

Rings and brooch

The clothes they wore were not quite the same as ours today, and they did not fit as well as ours do. They were fastened with different types of pins and brooches. Draw the modern equivalent of this Celtic brooch in the box below. *Clue*: babies usually have one.

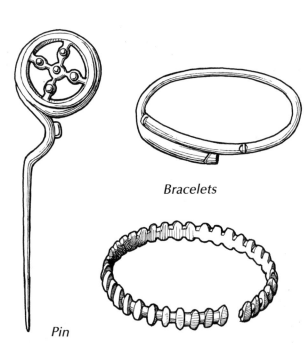

Bracelets

Pin

A PICTURE TO COLOUR

You will find lots of clues in this book
to help you fill in colours and patterns.
Add jewellery from the drawings on the
opposite page.

Celtic art

As well as jewellery and clothes, Celtic people loved beautifully made and decorated objects. Favourite or very important possessions, such as mirrors and weapons, must have taken great skill to make.

Most of the decorated objects which survive from Celtic times were made of metal — bronze, iron, gold and silver. Some of the decoration was *incised* (scratched) onto the surface of the object. Deeper lines were hammered in with a *punch*.

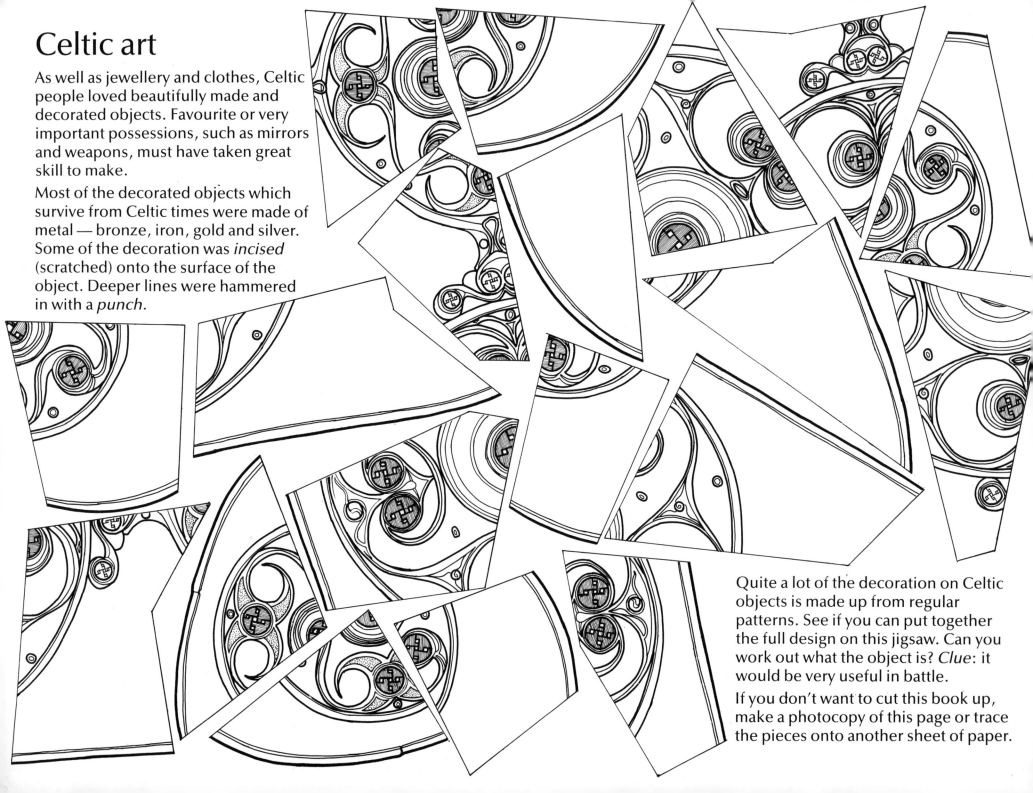

Quite a lot of the decoration on Celtic objects is made up from regular patterns. See if you can put together the full design on this jigsaw. Can you work out what the object is? *Clue*: it would be very useful in battle.

If you don't want to cut this book up, make a photocopy of this page or trace the pieces onto another sheet of paper.

DOT-TO-DOT
Join the dots to find a fantastic (or imaginary) animal which decorated a bucket.

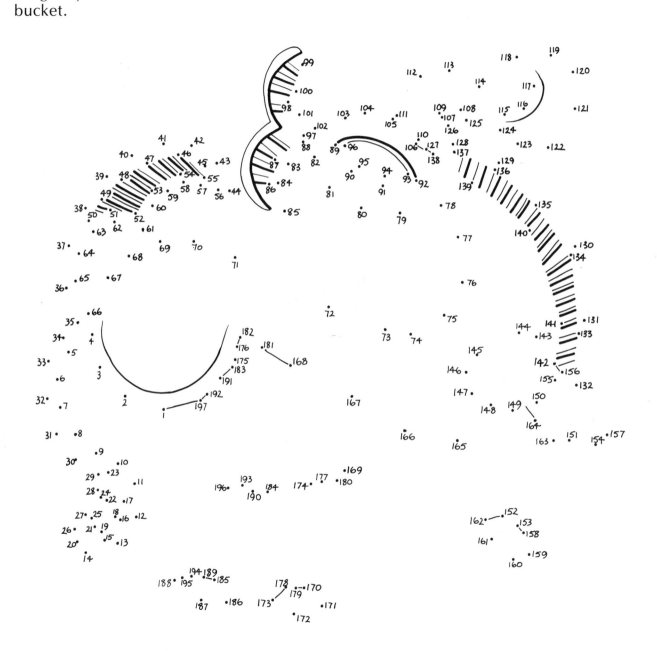

Here are some more Celtic patterns.
See if you can complete them.

Celtic religion

The Celts were very religious, but not quite in the same way as some people are today. They believed that gods and spirits were everywhere and could be dangerous to humans. Gods and spirits could work great magic and had to be worshipped, sometimes in special temples. Offerings (*sacrifices*) had to be made to them.

Celtic priests, called Druids, made sacrifices (sometimes human sacrifices) to the gods for the people. Shady oak-tree groves were favourite places for religious ceremonies. At certain times of the year, using sickles of gold, Druids would cut mistletoe from high up in the trees to use in the ceremonies.

WATER SACRIFICES
Especially after a great victory, the Celts would throw objects and victims (animals and people) into water as a gift to the gods. The most famous example of this is a group of objects which were found on the island of Mona, now called Anglesey. This island, off the north coast of Wales, was sacred to the Druids. The objects had been thrown into a pool.

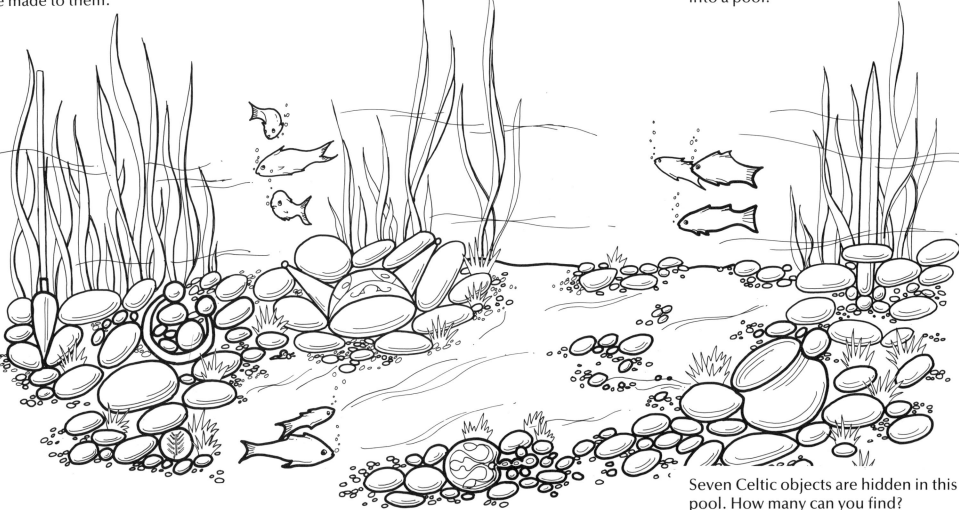

Seven Celtic objects are hidden in this pool. How many can you find?

CELTIC FESTIVALS

At certain times of the year Celtic peoples came together to worship and make sacrifices in great festivals. Do you know of any festivals which happen today on or near the same dates? We've given you the first letters of some which happen in Britain (answers on page 16). Maybe you know some which happen in other countries.

IN CELTIC TIMES	IN BRITAIN TODAY
SAMAIN (night of 31st October to 1st November) when all the spirits of the Other World were set loose on the human world. A time of great danger. The beginning of the Celtic year.	H - - - - - - -
BELTANE (1st May) when feasting, sacrificing and celebration took place to thank the gods for getting the people safely through the winter. It was also to help with fertility of crops and animals. A giant man of straw was burnt.	M - - D - -
LUGHNASA (15 days before 1st August and 15 days after) was a festival to celebrate the harvesting of the crops.	H - - - - - - F - - - - - - -

Another feast was sacred to the goddess Brigit (1st February) and was connected with the coming into milk of ewes (female sheep).

Animals were important in worship too. The heads of some animals were specially buried in pits in the ground. Can you work out what this skull came from? It's the same animal as on the Celtic coin next to it.

Animals

The Celts liked to decorate objects with animals. Here are some examples.

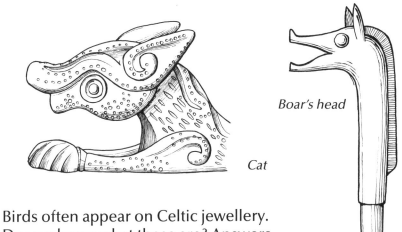

Cat

Boar's head

Birds often appear on Celtic jewellery. Do you know what these are? Answers on page 16.

Have you ever seen a horse cut into the hillside, like this one at Uffington in Oxfordshire?

Celtic coin

Druids...

Although the Celts didn't write things down, we know a lot about them from the *evidence* they left behind, which is investigated by archaeologists. We also know something about them from Greeks and Romans who wrote about them.

THE DRUIDS
Held religious ceremonies and made sacrifices

Tried people for crimes in court

Were responsible for passing on knowledge to the younger generation

Were responsible for calling the whole tribe together in an assembly each year (you will have to think about this one!)

WHAT DID DRUIDS LOOK LIKE?
We know what some Celtic people looked like and what sort of clothes they wore. There are plenty of examples in this book. But we don't know what Druids looked like or what they wore. They weren't just ordinary Celts, like warriors or farmers or metalworkers, and priests usually wear special clothes.

What do YOU think a Druid might have looked like? On the left is an outline for you to add to from your imagination, and to colour in.

The Romans have told us a little about the Druids. The Druids were very important people in Celtic tribes and they were more than just priests. Look below at the jobs the Druids did. Who does them today? Write your answers in the space below.

TODAY

Think about whether a Druid might have had:

A moustache?

Limed hair, or perhaps a special hat?

Trousers or a tunic? A cloak?

Shoes or bare feet? Rings on his toes?

Tattooes or woad-coloured patterns?

Jewellery?

... and Romans

ENTER THE ROMANS

The Celtic peoples were taken over by the Romans in a number of countries in the Roman Empire. In Britain, which they invaded in AD 43, the Romans soon overcame even the fierce Celtic warriors. Even so, there was still opposition to the Romans afterwards, especially from the Druids. The Romans hated the Druids, because they stirred the people up against them. Eventually, the Roman army massacred all the Druids, who had fled to their sacred island of Mona.

In AD 60, while the Roman commander Suetonius Paulinus was governor in Britain, there was a major revolt against Roman rule, led by the queen of the Iceni tribe in East Anglia. She was the famous Boudica. Her name means Victory, so she was really our first Queen Victoria. (There is a description of her on page 2.) But the revolt failed, and Boudica was killed.

Paulinus called the Celts 'savages'. Now you have read through this book, what do YOU think?

Which route will lead Paulinus to Boudica?

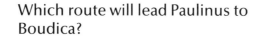

After the Celts

When the Romans came to Britain they often 'Romanised' (made Roman) the names of towns and other places. For example, they heard the word for 'the town in the woods' and wrote it down in Latin as Calleva. (That's the town now called Silchester, in Hampshire.) The name used for the whole country, Britain, was probably said by Celtic peoples as PRETANNIA. Greek and then Roman travellers made it BRITANNIA = Britain.

Some Celtic languages survived the Roman occupation (and later invasions by other peoples) of Britain and Europe. People still speak Celtic languages in several countries today. For example, BRETON is still spoken in Brittany in northern France, CORNISH in Cornwall and GAELIC in parts of Scotland and Ireland.

FINDING OUT MORE ABOUT THE CELTS
Prehistory by Keith Branigan (Kingfisher Books 1984) looks at the prehistoric peoples (including the Celts) in Europe.

The Penguin Guide to Prehistoric England and Wales by James Dyer (1981) is the best book to help you find Celtic sites to visit.

A good story to read about the Celts is *Sun Horse, Moon Horse* by Rosemary Sutcliffe (Macmillan 1981).

You can visit a reconstructed Celtic settlement complete with houses, crops and animals at Butser Ancient Farm in Queen Elizabeth Country Park, Horndean, near Petersfield, Hampshire.

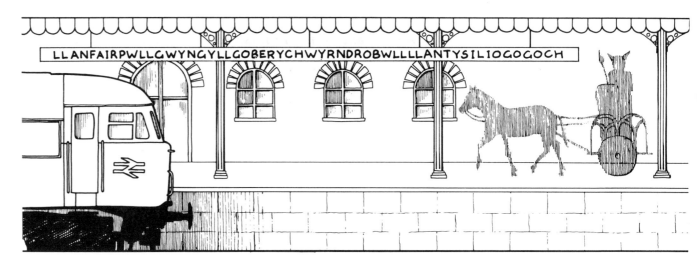

LLANFAIRPWLLGWYNGYLLGOBERYCHWYRNDROBWLLLLANTYSILIOGOGOCH

This railway station is WELSH, another language spoken today which connects us directly with Celtic peoples. The Celts might not be able to understand the whole word, though. It means 'St Mary's Church in a hollow of white hazel close to a rapid whirlpool and St Tysilio's Church'.

DO YOU HAVE A CELTIC NAME?
ALAN (or ALUN in Welsh) was introduced into Britain by Breton followers of William the Conqueror. GLADYS comes from GWLADYS, which is probably an Old Welsh version of the Roman name CLAUDIA.

CELTIC FIRST NAMES

BRIAN	DYLAN	MERLIN
BRYN	ENID	MORGAN
DEIRDRE	EMLYN	MORWENNA
DONALD	GARETH	MURIEL
DUNCAN	GAVIN	WALLACE

If you are called MARTIN, ADRIAN, ANTHONY, ANTONIA or OCTAVIA, you cannot claim to be Celtic. Those names all come from Roman names. Sorry!

ANSWERS
Page 5 Rabbits were not introduced into Britain until the Norman invasion in AD 1066. And of course the Celts did not have television!

Page 13 The festivals are Halloween, May Day and Harvest Festival. The birds are an owl and cormorants.

© 1989 The Trustees of the British Museum
Published by British Museum Press
a division of The British Museum Company Ltd
46 Bloomsbury Street, London WC1B 3QQ

Sixth impression 1995

ISBN 0-7141-1393-X

Drawings and back cover illustration by Amanda Balfour
Front cover illustration by William Webb

Typeset by Rowland Phototypesetting (London) Ltd
Printed in Great Britain by St Edmundsbury Press Ltd, Bury St Edmunds, Suffolk